ZOO
ANIMALS

Cathy Kilpatrick

TREASURE
PRESS

CONTENTS

Introduction 4

Africa 8

The Americas 18

Famous Zoos 32

Australasia 34

Eurasia 40

Southeast Asia 48

Polar Regions 56

Index 64

Orang-utans are protected in their jungle homes on the islands of Borneo and Sumatra. However, poachers still shoot the mothers to obtain the babies for 'black-market' dealings, and their forest habitat is rapidly being destroyed. Zoos conserve them (left) by breeding many most successfully.

INTRODUCTION

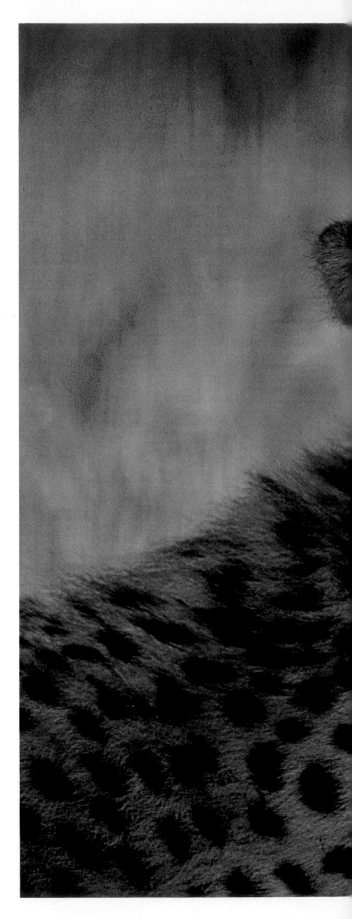

Zoos have been an attraction for thousands of years. The earliest zoo dates back to the kings of Old-Kingdom Egypt who ruled from 2900 to 2000 BC. They kept hyenas, monkeys, many kinds of antelopes and even mongooses. Later, temple gardens contained animals including leopards, cheetahs, tall kinds of cattle, exotic birds and giraffes brought from far-off places.

In China the royalty of these ancient times also built up animal collections. They had deer, various fishes and 'white birds with dazzling plumes'. The ancient Greeks were the first seriously to study their captive animals. From the seventh century BC they began to import monkeys from northern Africa and to tame them. In the next century they were keeping francolins which are a kind of partridge, cranes, purple gallinules and domestic cats from Africa. A hundred years later the spectacular peacock was brought from India.

Wealthy Romans certainly kept small private zoos in the gardens of their country villas by the first century BC. Various breeds of chickens, ducks, geese and pigeons were reared; though many were destined for the table. The Romans had large public menageries from the third century BC. They had arena shows of elephants where the huge beasts were trained to fight one another. The Romans were also famous for their spectacular fights and arena shows where bulls fought men, and lions and bears fought to the death. Later, of course, it was the Christians who filled the role. During the rule of Caesar Augustus (63 BC–AD 14) there was wanton slaughter of many exotic animals including tigers, lions, crocodiles, hippos, rhinos and leopards. These terrible arena bloodbaths went on almost continuously until the fall of the Roman Empire, when zoo collections declined throughout Europe.

In the 12th century, Henry I of England kept park cattle, lions, leopards, lynxes and camels in a small menagerie in Oxfordshire which was probably started by his father, William the Conqueror. Zoological collections began to increase from the turn of the 15th century onward as explorers ventured further to discover new lands. Columbus brought back the first macaws from the West Indies

The handsome spotted cheetah (right) is the fastest animal on land.

to Europe. During the 16th century cassowaries from Australia, turkeys from Mexico, and llamas and guinea-pigs from South America reached the menageries of the European nobility. The first chimpanzees arrived during the next century, as did the birds-of-paradise from New Guinea.

In 1624 a great zoo was founded at Versailles near Paris in France, by Louis XIII. This displayed many species of animals from distant lands including tapirs, hummingbirds, toucans and cardinals from America and lemurs from Madagascar. The oldest of the zoos of the world to survive to this day is Schönbrunn Zoo in Austria. It was built by Francis I for his wife Maria Theresa in 1752. Another old surviving zoo is the famous Jardin des Plantes, Paris, which was founded in 1793 to exhibit animals as well as house the first medicinal plant collection.

There are not many old zoos to be found in the United States. This is because the pioneers con-centrated on the conservation of wild animals in their natural habitats. Yellowstone National Park was founded for this purpose. Bison, elk, bears, moose and mountain sheep are found in this huge natural park in Montana, USA.

The first modern zoos of the 19th century showed animals mainly to allow people to see strange creatures from far-off countries. They took little account of the animals' comfort. There was a great furore in 1835 at the London Zoo when it received its first chimpanzee, and again 15 years later when the first hippopotamus was put on exhibit. All London flocked to see these amazing animals. The word zoo in fact was coined at this time; it comes from a popular Victorian music-hall song which included the lyrics 'Walking in the zoo is the okay thing to do!' London Zoo can be said to be the oldest surviving example of a proper zoological garden, as opposed to groups of animals being exhibited in a

Natural surroundings are often mimicked in captivity to make the animals feel more at home. Here prairie dogs can dig underground runs to form 'towns' in their enclosures (above).

White tigers (left) were first exhibited and bred in Delhi Zoo: a white male cub had been caught in an Indian forest in 1952.

menagerie with no regard for natural features.

Today, the aims of most modern zoos involve more than just the entertainment of the public. They wish to instruct and educate their visitors and the majority have good education departments and children's zoos. Another aim is to carry out zoological research and protect wild animal life. This may seem a contradiction at first. However, with the disappearance of some of the world's wild habitats, many animal species are endangered. By keeping and breeding these species in zoos their survival is ensured. In some cases, where the animal has almost disappeared in the wild, captive specimens have been bred so successfully that numbers of them have been released back into the wild. This is the case with the Hawaiian goose or ne-ne. White rhinos, orang-utangs, white tigers, and pygmy chimpanzees and gorillas were all endangered in the wild but are now being bred successfully in modern zoos. Animals in zoos are now rarely kept in closed and stuffy conditions as they once were, but are given as much space and fresh air as possible. Barriers are no longer the thick iron-bar type or heavy close mesh but are as invisible and unobtrusive as possible. Water-filled moats, walk-through aviaries and mixed compatible collections are some of the new designs and exhibits that are seen.

AFRICA

A wealth of fascinating and exotic animals comes from various parts of Africa. Many are favourites in zoos including the lions (*below*). Lions are no longer taken from their African grassland home for zoos because they breed so well in captivity. A female gives birth to between three and six cubs.

Africa is the home of a multitude of birds, many of them very colourful and some quite large. The crowned crane (*left*) is a favourite because, although shy and wary in its grassland savannah home, it settles down well in captivity. Usually this tall, graceful bird has its wings clipped and is allowed to walk around the zoo grounds.

The curious secretary bird (*above*) searches the grass for snakes, small mammals, insects and lizards. It pounds a snake to death with its feet while holding it in its bill and protecting itself from any snake bite with outstretched wings. In zoological collections it eats freshly killed small rodents and insects. The secretary bird is so called because of the feathers of its head which stick out behind, like the quill pens that secretaries in Dickensian times would tuck behind their ears.

The largest bird living today is the ostrich (*right*) and a male can stand almost 2·5m (8ft) tall. This bird is unable to fly but when attacked or chased it will either kick out with its strong feet, or run away at high speed.

The monkeys and apes are always a huge attraction to visitors in a zoo. Most monkeys and baboons have always bred well in captivity and the spectacular blue-and-red-faced mandrill, a ground-dwelling baboon, is no exception. A mother (*below*) caresses her young infant with great care and love. Her face is not as colourful as the male's, although it is still an important social signal. These baboons, which come from the low-lying forests of equatorial West Africa, have vividly coloured hind-quarters and buttocks, especially in the male.

The gorilla is the largest living primate. A large male weighs up to 200kg (450lb). Probably the most famous one in the world was Guy the Gorilla (*right*) who lived at London Zoo from 1947–78. Although they look very strong and aggressive, in the wild gorillas are shy, gentle creatures, living in family groups led by an old male, called a silverback because of his greying hair. Mainly vegetarian, gorillas are fed in zoos on a specially mixed diet which is supplemented with fruit, green vegetables and milk.

The African elephant (*below*) is distinguished from its Asian cousin by much larger ears. Also, at the end of the long, sensitive trunk, there are two 'fingers', one above and one below the nostrils. An Asian elephant has only one finger, situated above the nostril (*see endpapers*).

The long-nosed African crocodile (*right*) is quick to move when food arrives, although it can remain motionless for hours on end.

The white rhino (*below right*) and black rhino are the two species of African rhinoceros, the former of which is quite rare in the wild.

The average giraffe is almost as tall as a double-decker bus – the record height is 6.3m (19ft 2in). Giraffe houses must therefore be very high, like this one at the London Zoo (*left*). In countries with cold winters, heating must be provided for the animals. Wild giraffes browse on the leaves, twigs and branches of trees such as the acacia tree of the savannah. In captivity they are provided mainly with clover hay as well as fresh vegetables and branches of evergreen oak. This is placed in a high feeding trough. Giraffes chew the cud. They feed quickly, and then a few hours later while they are resting each ball of partly digested food is brought back up the gullet for a second thorough chewing, just as in cows.

The only close relative of the giraffe is the okapi (*right*). It is found in the dense tropical equatorial forests of Africa and is one of the least-known large mammals, due to its shy, solitary nature. The few zoos that have them, such as Frankfurt zoo, encourage them to breed.

Zebras breed well in zoos and it is no longer necessary to take specimens from the wild such as this Burchell's zebra and foal (*below*), feeding in Etosha National Park. Why they have a striped coat is still something of a mystery. Perhaps the effect of the stripes causes a lion to misjudge its pounce, or, at a distance in the heat haze, they blend in with the surroundings.

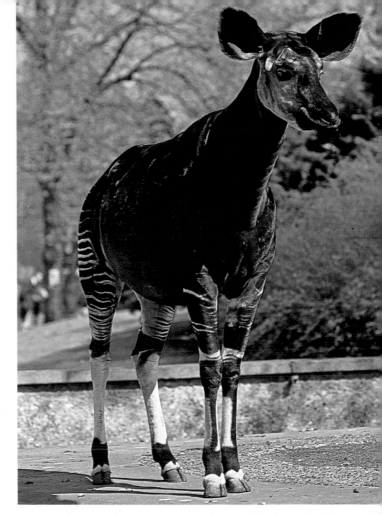

THE AMERICAS

Ambling anteaters, amusing armadillos and gigantic anacondas all come from the South American continent, while dramatic skunks, battling beavers and browsing bison make North America their home. Hummingbirds such as the one shown here are the dazzling jewels of the tropics of America. Hovering in one spot, they use their beak and tongue to suck nectar from flowers.

The three-toed sloth (*above*), with its cousin the two-toed sloth, is the slowest moving mammal living today. Its life is spent hanging on long, curved claws from a branch, reluctantly moving in order to obtain fruit or leaves. It is a good swimmer if it loses its hold and falls into a waterway in its tropical rainforest home, such as the Amazon basin. However, if it falls to the ground it is almost helpless. Its fur has a greenish tinge, caused by algae growing on the strands of its hair. This provides camouflage.

The mammal with the most brilliantly coloured coat is the golden lion marmoset (*right*) which gets its name from the long mane fringing its face. Marmosets and tamarins are the Lilliputians of the monkey kingdom, living in social family groups in the tropical forests of South America. They keep in contact with one another by means of high-pitched twitters and squeaks. Some monkey voices are almost bird-like, such as that of the curious cottontop (*left*) which was one of the first South American monkeys to reach Europe.

Most monkeys give birth to a single baby, but marmosets and tamarins usually give birth to twins. It is an interesting and unusual fact that the father cares for the babies most of the time, carrying them around his shoulders and neck like a scarf. He hands them over to their mother at feeding time.

Armadillos are the only mammals to have a shell. It is not solid like a tortoise's but is made from groups of large scales joined together in bony segments. Some scales form bands that are connected with muscles and skin, allowing the armadillo both protection and flexiblility. The hairy armadillo (*above*), like its relatives, is a powerful digger and lives in the burrows it excavates. If attacked, it will at first try to run away and then attempt to burrow. If this fails it draws in its feet so that the edges of its armour are in contact with the ground, so protecting it from predators such as the Pampas fox.

The giant anteater (*right*) should probably be called the giant termite-eater as it prefers to eat these. It rips open termite nests with its powerful front claws and licks up the eggs, cocoons and adult termites on its long sticky tongue which shoots in and out very rapidly. In captivity the giant anteaters are fed on a special mixture of eggs, mince, vitamins and ants' eggs.

The anaconda can grow to 9m (30ft) and is the main contender for the title of largest of all living snakes (*top right*). Some people believe that the Asian reticulated python holds this record, however (see page 53). In zoos the anaconda does not usually reach more than 6.5m (20ft) in length.

The tropical rainforests of South America are the home of many colourful birds. One of the most brilliant and dazzling is the Peruvian cock-of-the-rock. It is only the male bird (*left*) that is brightly feathered, the female being drab in colour. In the breeding season the male dances and postures in a display area in order to attract a mate. As he displays, his crest is fanned forward to hide his bill. After a female has chosen her partner and mated, she flies some distance to build a mud nest in a sheltered area. Here she lays, incubates and rears her young by herself.

The blue-and-yellow macaw (*below left*) is a favourite in zoos because often it says 'hello' and a few other words taught to it by its keepers. However, the curved sharp beak can crack Brazil nuts with ease, so fingers should never be offered to this bird. Macaws come from the tropical forests of Central and South America, and move about in pairs or in family groups.

Macaws belong to the parrot family and, like all its members, they have two toes pointing forwards and two toes pointing backwards. This assists the birds when climbing about branches or when holding fruit or nuts. The blue-and-yellow macaw is one of the largest of all American parrots.

Toucans have huge, bizarre bills that are rivalled only by those of the hornbills of Africa and Asia. The bill is not as ungainly or as heavy as it appears. The horny outer layer is supported by a network of bony filaments; the rest is just space. The beak is therefore very light but amazingly strong. The birds will delicately pick up a berry or small fruit with the tip and then with a flick of the head the food is tossed into the mouth. It will also take insects, spiders and the occasional lizard or small bird nestling. The reason for the colourful beak is a mystery, but perhaps it is used to identify its own kind or in display. The red-billed toucan (*right*), however, feeds almost exclusively on fruit.

If a toucan damages its bill-tip then its ability to feed is severely hampered. In one zoo, their prize toucan lost the tip of its lower bill. The bird was saved when its keeper carefully moulded the beak to its original shape.

The striped skunk (*overleaf*) is found only in North America in the temperate forests. Here it survives by foraging in leaf litter on the forest floor for insects and grubs, and it also enjoys the occasional mouse, bird's egg or piece of carrion. In the photograph the skunk looks as if it is in the wild, but this is an example of an excellent enclosure for this captive animal. When disturbed the skunk will use its anal glands and eject foul-smelling liquid over its attacker.

The beaver in captivity (*below*) needs a large pool with access to trees or logs so it can build its own lodge or add to a man-made one. It spends much time oiling and grooming its fur which is water-repellent. When the beaver swims its tail acts as a rudder and can give a resounding warning slap on the surface of the water when the beaver is diving from danger.

A raccoon in captivity (*right*) is said to wash its food in its water-dish. This habit is a result of the enclosed conditions. In the wild, the animal instinctively searches shallow waters for crayfish and this behaviour is automatically carried out in captivity.

The North American tree-porcupine (*below right*) has long coarse hairs which hide its needle-sharp quills.

The American bison (*below*) is sometimes called a buffalo. It used to roam the vast prairies of North America, but during the 19th century these massive ox-like beasts were slaughtered in their millions as European settlers pushed west across the continent. Numbering 50 million at the beginning of the 19th century, by 1889 there were only 540 left. The settlers killed them for meat and hides. Also, large-scale hunts were organized to feed the men building the railroads. 'Buffalo Bill' Cody was a professional hunter of these times. It became a sport to shoot as many bison as possible: one man killed over 100 beasts in a day, leaving the carcases to rot. It is true that the bison was the mainstay of the American Indian tribes but they accounted for the death of relatively few when compared to the killing by settlers and hunters.

Before the last ones were killed conservation-minded people took action and saved the impressive beasts from extinction. Today the American bison is found breeding well in most zoos. In America it survives in the wild in large national parks where numbers have reached 50,000.

The American bison is more massive than its European cousin. It has a heavy head, thick shaggy hair over the front of its body, and humped shoulders. It stands up to 3m (9ft 8in) high.

The grizzly bear (*right*) has a most ferocious reputation and this is basically well-founded. It is big, beautiful, powerful and totally unpredictable in its Arctic tundra home of North America. The grizzly is a race of the brown bear species which is found not only in North America but also Eurasia. This race is much larger than most brown bears, a large male weighing up to 450kg (990lb).

In the wild the grizzly eats anything from fruit and berries to small lemmings, migrating salmon and the occasional caribou. It does not hug its prey to death as is popularly believed. The bear strikes large prey with its powerful front legs and then rips the victim open with its long curved sharp claws. In captivity it is fed with a mixed diet. Although feeding is not permitted in most zoos – the animals get all they need from their keepers – many grizzlies, as well as other bears, have developed the habit of standing up on their hind legs to beg from the public. A grizzly in this position stands over 2m (6ft 6in) tall.

Also from North America is the related black bear. It is quite difficult to tell a black from a brown bear as both species can range in colour from light brown to jet black. However, black bears are usually smaller than brown bears and less bulky in appearance.

FAMOUS ZOOS

Every year millions of people visit hundreds of zoos around the world. Many of these zoos concentrate on entertaining and educating the visitors, researching on animals within their collection and conserving and breeding the rarer species of animals. Here are just a few of the excellent zoos you can visit.

THE BRONX, NEW YORK, ZOOLOGICAL PARK, USA

This 225-acre zoo, opened in 1899, is famous for its architectural designs and good breeding successes. It was one of the first zoos to present mixed exhibits of animals in new large enclosures. The first one was the African Plains area. This zoo carries out its three main aims extremely well. The first aim is that it should be a feature of New York's cultural life, letting the public see life within nature. The second is that it should be a focus for education and research, where man can know life within nature. The third is that the zoo should be a force for the conservation of wild life, so that man can conserve life within nature. The zoo is famous for acquiring and maintaining rarities among its collection. Notable zoo 'firsts' include pygmy hippopotamus, duck-billed platypus, vampire bat, gorilla, King penguin and the Komodo dragon. The zoo has a huge nocturnal house for night-active animals and a beautiful tropical bird house.

SAN DIEGO ZOO, CALIFORNIA, USA

Due to the climate and weather being consistently agreeable, the animals of this zoo can live outdoors almost all the year round. It is a most impressive zoo containing one of the largest and rarest collections of animals in the world. It exceeds most other zoos in the number of animals and species exhibited. San Diego also has a marvellous plant, shrub and tree collection. A bus ride can be taken through the 128 acres before a visitor chooses which houses to visit. In the children's zoo there is a nursery for orphan animals and youngsters are allowed to help the staff at times.

LONDON ZOOLOGICAL GARDENS, REGENTS PARK, ENGLAND

Hundreds of different animals are to be found in this 36-acre zoo, many of them, such as the giant pandas and apes, attracting large crowds. The prime exhibits are Ching-Ching and Chia-Chia, the giant panda successors to Chi-Chi, Lein-ho and Ming. Gradually the old Victorian cages are being replaced by modern, well-designed animal houses, with a large cat exhibit and an education department being the most recent modernizations. The Snowdon Aviary, a walk-through aviary opened in 1965, still attracts attention. Visitors walk across a cantilever bridge and get a bird's eye view of ducks, herons and other inmates.

Whipsnade Zoo, near Dunstable, Bedfordshire also belongs to the Zoological Society. Within its 550 acres large groups of animals live in surroundings as natural as possible. A breeding herd of rare white rhinos can be observed from a train which passes through their enclosure. A small dolphinarium is another fairly recent structure.

TARONGA PARK ZOOLOGICAL GARDENS, SYDNEY, AUSTRALIA

Some 70 acres of zoological park are to be found behind a Disney-style main gate. The zoo specializes in animals native to Australia, and exhibits the best collection of marsupials in the world. Many of the animal pens have concrete floors that can be washed daily and scattered with new clean cover. This reduces infection by the internal parasites present in an animal's droppings. A main attraction is the platypusary and observation room for underwater viewing of the duck-billed platypus, an egg-laying monotreme unique to the continent. This zoo has had many noted breeding successes, particularly with black rhinos, kiwis and koala bears.

FRANKFURT ZOO, WEST GERMANY
The director of this zoo is Bernhard Grzimek, wildlife conservationist and film maker who is especially interested in African animals. The new idea of walk-through aviaries was developed here (as well as at San Diego); these make more natural space available for the birds and also provide closer contact between people and animals. For the 3,000-square-metre (3,600-square-yard) enclosure for grassland animals, the architects and zoological staff worked out the critical dimensions and shape so that, when landscaped, it enabled gazelles, blesboks, ostriches and bustards all to live in harmony within the one enclosure. There is a small isolated hill that the herd leader of the blesboks uses as a look-out post. As a result of the near-natural way in which the animals live, the zoo has an excellent breeding record.

VINCENNES, PARC ZOOLOGIQUE DE PARIS, FRANCE
This large park was opened in 1934 to accommodate large groups and herds of animals within its 42 acres. The *Rocher* is the centre of the zoo. This is an artificial mountain rising about 40 metres (145 ft) into the air, with paths winding around its white rocks to the peak. Around the base are pools with various species of penguins, and the heights are the home of mountain goats. An elevator within the structure takes visitors to the peak from where they can see Paris stretching to the horizon in all directions. This is one of the few zoos to have developed a true, captive-bred stock of okapis.

PEKING ZOO, CHINA
This zoo is world famous for being the only one to breed giant pandas in captivity. It always has several of these native animals on display and they are the prize exhibit. These animals are given impressive housing and enclosures: they live in very large air-conditioned houses behind glass, which have rocks, pools, bedding material and intermittent water sprays. The pandas can leave their indoor area to wander in large outdoor enclosures where the grassy banks are planted with clumps of bamboo and mimosa trees. The animals like to spend the cool early mornings and late evenings outside. The zoo bred its first giant pandas in 1963. The zoo also has a most impressive collection of breeds of goldfish and koi carp. The Chinese were the first to domesticate goldfish more than 1,000 years ago.

TOKYO ZOO, JAPAN
Established in 1882, Ueno Zoological Gardens cover 32 acres with 450 species on show. It is a large major collection limited, as in London, by space. As a result, in 1958 it established the Tama Zoological Park which covers 84 acres outside the city. The older main zoo is one of the most visited in the world, with nearly four million people passing through it every year.

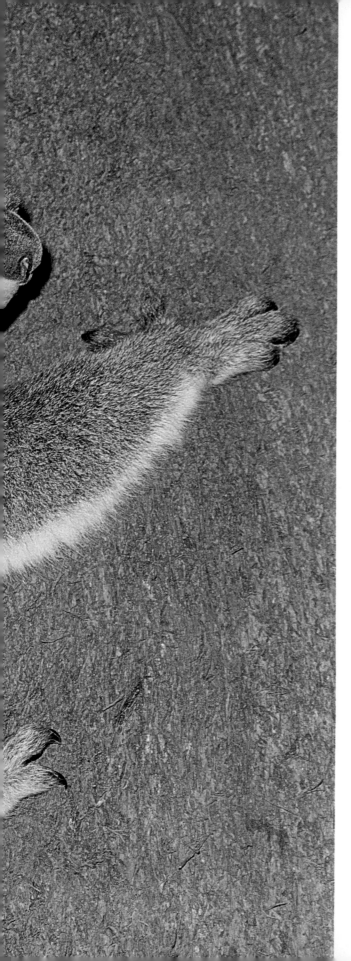

AUSTRALASIA

The majority of animals from Australia, New Zealand and the other islands of the region are truly distinct from the fauna of the rest of the world. This is because they have been cut off by the seas from other continents for 50 million years.

Australia and New Guinea are the only places on Earth where the three basic types of mammals exist side by side: the monotremes, the marsupials and the placentals. The greatest difference between them is in the way they reproduce. Monotremes lay eggs and only two kinds survive today: the duck-billed platypus and the echidna or spiny anteater. In marsupials the young are born at an age when they are very small and only partly developed. The young embryo-like babies find their way almost unaided to the mother's pouch and latch onto a teat. They feed for a long time until they are fully developed. Kangaroos, koalas, wallabies, sugar gliders and wombats are all marsupials. The koala (*left*) is rarely found in zoos outside Australia because it feeds on leaves of species of native eucalyptus trees. The placental mammal is the most advanced and successful as it has developed the placenta in the womb which allows the exchange of gases and provides nourishment for growth so that the babies are well developed at birth.

The sulphur-crested cockatoo (*left*) is one of the many species of parrot that live in Australia. This bird causes great amusement to zoo visitors as not only will it often say 'hello' and other simple words, but it also raises its yellow crest as a greeting. If you nod your head at a sulphur-crested cockatoo and then move your head from side to side the bird will respond and do similar actions. In the wild this behaviour is part of the bird's courtship display.

The kiwi (*top right*) is found only on the islands of New Zealand. There are three species but they are very difficult to tell apart. This flightless chicken-sized bird is nocturnal, hiding during the day in a well-protected burrow that it usually makes among the roots of trees. The wings of a kiwi probably enabled the bird to fly millions of years ago but now they are hidden by the bird's loose, shaggy plumage. Because of the lack of predators native to New Zealand, the ability to fly was not essential for the kiwis' survival. The long down-curved beak has nostrils at its tip which enable the bird to smell worms and insects in the leaf-litter and surface soil of the forest.

Two species of flightless bird that live on the Australian continent are often seen in zoos. These are the emu and the cassowary. The emu is the largest bird in Australia and is second in size to the ostrich. Over much of their dry, savannah, grass-land home they have been persecuted and shot, so the emu is seldom seen in the wild. The cassowary (*bottom right*) is one of the most shy and wary of all tropical rainforest birds. It is a strange-looking bird with its helmet and coloured wattles. The reason for its helmet, which is a large bony crest, is not understood; it may function as a protective shield as the bird pushes its way through the undergrowth of the rain-forest, or it could be for recognizing its own species, or it may play a part in breeding behaviour. At the moment no one knows. The cassowary has a decorative wattle hanging from its throat, and long, drooping, tough feathers which help protect it from the thorny undergrowth of its native habitat.

The cassowary normally feeds on fruit, insects and plants. It has been known for a man to be killed with a kick of the bird's powerful legs which have sharp curved claws on each foot. Keepers are always on their guard when inside the enclosure of a cassowary.

The platypus (*left*) is confined to eastern Australia where it is far more common in slow-flowing streams, rivers and reservoirs than most people believe. It is rare to find the creature exhibited in zoos apart from Australian ones, as it has such a specialized diet. It detects freshwater invertebrates, such as yabbies, a kind of small crayfish, with its sensitive beak. It needs an aquatic habitat with soft banks so that it can dig out burrows. A mated female will lay two eggs in a burrow. These hatch into blind, naked babies in two to three weeks. They lap milk which ouzes from special pores on the mother's abdomen.

The grey kangaroo (*below*) adapts well to living in zoos. A female can often be spotted with her young poking out of her pouch. The baby is called a joey and it lives in the pouch until it is too heavy for the mother to carry it.

The vegetarian wombat is a powerful digger; its stocky build and shovel-like claws enable it to dig long, deep burrows. The hairy-nosed wombat (*top right*) comes from South Australia.

The Tasmanian devil (*bottom right*), as its name suggests, is found only on the island of Tasmania. It is a large, powerfully built flesh-eater, hunting small mammals and reptiles. Some kill weakened sheep and they are therefore not liked by farmers.

EURASIA

Few Europeans have seen the native animals of Eurasia, such as wolves, brown bears, red foxes, red deer, golden eagles or common bustards, in their wild homes. However, most zoos exhibit these animals and the majority of them have been born and bred in captivity so that the wild fauna of Eurasia is not reduced any further. Brown bears (*below*), once common throughout Eurasia, are now numerous only in the Balkans and Russia.

Père David's deer (*above*), named after the French naturalist, have been park and zoo deer for centuries. All of those alive today are descended from a herd kept in the Chinese emperor's hunting park near Peking which was discovered by Père David in 1856. The Chinese describe the animal as having reindeer hoofs, stag antlers, a camel's neck and a donkey's tail, but to most onlookers it is a handsome animal. Its broad hoofs are adapted for walking in swampy and marshy ground, as in its former range on the low-lying plains and river flats of China. It swims very well and will spend long periods standing in mud. Only the stags have antlers which they shed after the rut, the breeding season. There are no more than 700 Père David's deer in the world today.

The saiga antelope (*right*) is a curious-looking animal with prominent bulbous nostrils. In the 1930s there were only a few hundred of these antelopes surviving on the grassland steppes of southeast Russia and central Asia. They were being shot to obtain the short horns of the male which fetched high prices in China where they were ground down for medicinal purposes. Hunting was banned and the numbers increased at an extremely rapid rate and its range widened. Today there are more than two and a half million saiga antelopes. Scientists discovered that the high birth-rate was due to the fact that females can give birth when only one year old, and half of them give birth to twins. Adult saigas are about 75cm (2ft 6in) high.

One of the most impressive sights in any bird-of-prey collection is the regal golden eagle (*left*). In the wild it lives in remote, inaccessible places such as the mountain regions of Europe, Asia and North America. Its range and numbers are severely diminished as farmers shot the eagle in the belief that it preyed on lambs. Also, many birds died when they fed on animals poisoned by pesticides. There is no proof that the eagle takes living lambs or fawns, but it will feed on corpses. The hooked bill of the golden eagle is extremely powerful and is used with the sharp talons of the feet to rip pieces of flesh from the prey. This can be seen at feeding time in zoos. Like all birds of prey, the eyesight of the golden eagle is excellent and extremely sharp. The eyes face forwards near the front of the head which gives the bird excellent binocular vision, vital in judging distances. When the eagle swoops down to snatch up a chosen victim in its talons it rarely misses.

The golden eagle is perhaps the best known of all the eagles in the world; it is also one of the largest with a wingspan of about 2m (6ft 6in).

Birds of prey are not the only ones to decline in numbers because of pressures put on them by man. Many species of bustard, medium to large ground-living birds with long powerful legs, are severely threatened because their chosen habitat has been taken over for agricultural land and the expansion of towns and cities. The great bustard of Europe (*below*) has disappeared from many of its former haunts including those in Great Britain, and is only found in sizable numbers in central and western Asia. In Britain it was extinct before 1850. Breeding programmes are being carried out at present in the hope that numbers will be increased to the point where the bustards can be reintroduced into suitable wild habitats such as the Salisbury Plain, England.

The great bustard is the largest flying land bird, a large male reaching around 15kg (33lb). The courtship display of a male is an astounding spectacle. He struts and stamps before a female, then shakes his plumage, raises his tail and twists his wings to expose white underfeathers.

The European bison or wisent (*below*) almost suffered the same fate as the American bison. It declined in numbers, not because it was shot indiscriminately, but because of the forest clearance in Europe where it lived. By the beginning of the 20th century the only surviving wild herd was in the Bialowieza Forest in Poland. In 1914 there were over 700 animals in this herd, but by the end of World War I not one was alive. Fortunately there were still a few in various European zoos and these were brought together to form a breeding nucleus in semi-captive conditions in the Bialowieza. World War II also took its toll and about 50 still survived. However, they were successfully bred in Poland and in many zoos. The wisent stands higher at the shoulder than the American bison, has a longer, less barrel-shaped body, and longer legs. Its head is smaller and is carried higher. Today the wisent is not in any danger of dying out.

The Eurasian common otter (*right*), although shy and wary in the wild and seldom seen, is unperturbed by human onlookers in captivity. A pair will spend hours chasing. diving and playing in and around their pool. In the wild the use of pesticides has caused a severe decline in otter numbers as the fish the otters eat and the water they swim in is poisoned.

Przewalski's horse (*below right*) is the last wild horse living on the steppes of central Asia. Some believe it no longer survives there but there are several breeding units to be found in zoos around the world and these number over 200 beasts. International efforts are being made to raise from this stock enough horses so that the species can be reintroduced into a national park or sanctuary on the steppes at some future date. The domesticated horse is descended from this stocky, erect-maned animal.

SOUTHEAST ASIA

Thought by many to be the most handsome of all the big cats, the tiger is perhaps the symbol for all wildlife in southeast Asia. In the past tigers have been hunted and shot as prized trophies so that they are now an endangered species in the wild. Most of the eight races are protected. Over 2,000 Indian or Bengal tigers (*below*) survive in the wild with a large breeding stock in zoos around the world. The tiger population is thought to be on the increase again, due mainly to the efforts of the World Wildlife Fund.

In many zoological gardens the peacock (*left*) is often seen freely strutting and wandering around the grounds. It is the male that has the wonderful eyed feathers which he raises into a fan to court a female (peahen). Although this fan is usually called his tail, in fact it is formed from greatly elongated tail couverts, not tail feathers. The less showy peahen lacks the train and her body plumage is a grey-brown. The blue or common peacock comes from India and Ceylon where it is an important symbol in religion and folktales. When we speak of someone as being 'proud as a peacock' it is because we have seen reflected in the peacock's display some of man's vanity for giving himself airs and graces. The peacock has been domesticated for centuries.

The pheasant family contains some of the most beautiful birds in the avian kingdom; their range of colours and shimmering feathers is matched only by the birds-of-paradise and humming birds. Many kinds are usually found in zoological collections including the silver pheasant, Impeyan pheasant, Lady Amherst pheasant and the golden pheasant, all from various districts in southeast Asia. The golden pheasant (*above*) originates from the highlands of central China. The male, as in all species of pheasant, has the magnificent plumage. His golden crest is raised in courtship and his other feathers are puffed up. The drab-coloured female incubates her eggs alone and rears her young. Her dull plumage helps to protect her from predators.

The flying frog (*below*) of the jungles of southeast Asia does not really fly. But it does glide from a high tree trunk down perhaps 15 to 20m (50 to 65ft) to the base of a distant tree. It can do this because its toes and fingers are fully webbed, so that when stretched they act like wing membranes. The star-shaped pupils, which expand in weak light, are probably an adaptation for finding food in the dimly lit jungle foliage.

Probably the largest snake in the world, large specimens of the reticulated python (*right*) can reach about 10m (32ft) and weigh 135kg (298lb). This python is, like all pythons and boas, a constricting type. It catches its victim with sharp fangs and coils its body around the struggling prey, squeezing it until it can no longer breathe. Then the prey is swallowed whole. In captivity snakes are fed on freshly killed prey such as rats and mice.

Today tapirs are found only in South America and southeast Asia. The Malyan tapir (*below*) has a striking black and white body. Standing about a metre (39in) high when fully grown, this animal uses its long mobile snout to browse on jungle foliage. It loves water and in captivity it is a frequent visitor to its pool. Young tapirs of all species have whitish-yellow spots and stripes over their dark coats and gain the normal adult coat between six and eight months after birth. The coat pattern of babies may be to conceal them in the dappled light of the jungle or it may be so that the adult can recognize her offspring.

Giant pandas are always a major attraction at the few zoos in the world fortunate enough to have them in their collection. These bear-like creatures (*right*) are most closely related to the raccoons of America. Giant pandas live in the mountains of western China where they feed on bamboo shoots, bulbs of alpine plants and small animals they catch. The Chinese people are carefully conserving these rare animals and it is thought their numbers are increasing. A full-grown giant panda measures about 1·8m (6ft) long. Its thick black and white coat gives it protection against the cold snows, as well as natural camouflage.

China is the only country that has bred these charming animals in captivity. The first living giant panda to be seen in the western world was in 1936 when Mrs Ruth Harkness brought the cub Su-lin, which she had collected in Szechwan, to America. Ming was the first giant panda to reach Britain, in 1938, and large crowds flocked to the London Zoo. The Chinese Government presented the giant pandas Ching-Ching and Chia-Chia to the London Zoo in 1974 and it is hoped that they can be bred during the 1980s. A female can breed when she is seven years old and the pair at London Zoo are being carefully studied and cared for in the hope that they may produce the first baby giant panda to be born outside China.

Although from the same area as the giant panda, the closely related red panda (*below*) is suited to a tree-dwelling life rather than a life on the ground. It lives on fruit, leaves, small mammals and birds. Like the giant panda it has 'six fingers'. These are special pads on the front paws which help the animal to hold bamboo shoots. During the day the red panda rests curled up in the fork of a tree, its bushy tail round its body like a scarf. It moves about during the night, searching for its food. It is found in greater numbers than the giant panda.

POLAR REGIONS

The polar regions of the world are inhospitable areas with freezing temperatures and snow and ice for most of the year. The northern polar region within the Arctic circle has more animal life than the South Pole as there is land mass surrounding the Arctic Ocean that becomes unfrozen during the short summer. The Antarctic land mass of the South Pole is permanently frozen, the ice being more than 3,000m (9,500ft) thick in places.

The largest and strongest predator of the Arctic circle is the polar bear (*previous page*), an adult male reaching over 450kg (992lb) in weight. However, it is a most agile carnivore, able to leap over crevasses some 3m (10ft) or more wide, and it can jump from one ice floe to another. This bear will hunt for seals, catching them unawares at breathing holes in the ice and dragging them out with teeth and curved claws, or stealthily creeping over the ice to surprise a basking seal, relying on its whie coat as camouflage. It will also eat smaller mammals such as lemmings and will gorge itself on berries such as billberries during the late summer on the Arctic tundra. It is an expert swimmer.

Polar bears breed well in captivity and the wild population is strictly protected these days. It is no longer possible to hunt this beautiful animal with a gun from helicopters, a sport that was becoming extremely popular with trophy hunters.

The Arctic fox (*below*) is also protected by its coat. During the winter the white coat hides this carnivore against the snow, and in summer it moults to brown fur. There is a dense woolly layer of undercoat hair and a longer coat of guard hairs.

Arctic foxes sometimes trail polar bears in the hope that they will be able to feed on the carcases of the bears' kills. During the summer, foxes eat mainly lemmings caught on the Arctic tundra.

The wolf (*right*) once lived in almost every land north of the tropical forests around the equator. Today, after centuries of persecution, its main stronghold is the Arctic tundra and the fringes of northern coniferous forests. It usually hunts in a small family pack, taking mainly caribou and weak musk-oxen. It does not hibernate in the winter months so must hunt or starve. Despite their reputation as enemies of man, wolves rarely attack human beings unless provoked.

The snowy owl of the far north is a most beautiful bird. It depends mainly on lemmings for food. About every fourth year the lemming population is very large and the owl is able to produce up to 12 nestlings rather than the 2 or 3 of years when the lemming population is small. The female (*below*) has more speckles and bars on her coat and she is bigger than her mate. The patterned coat helps conceal her as she incubates her eggs in the ground-nest among the lichens and grasses of the Arctic tundra. The male has an almost completely white plumage. These attractive birds of prey are found in many zoos and breed quite well in captivity. They are large birds, with a wingspan of about 1.2m (4ft).

The harp seal, sometimes known as the Greenland seal or saddleback, is found in the extreme northern parts of the Atlantic and nearby areas of the Arctic Ocean. The day-old pup (*right*) is known as a 'whitecoat', this stiff woolly coat being shed after three to four weeks. Each year sealers are allowed by law to cull certain numbers of whitecoats and these actions cause great concern to wildlife lovers and conservationists.

The caribou of North America (*below*) is the same animal as the reindeer in Europe. Barren-ground caribou of the North American tundra make annual journeys between northern summer haunts and forested areas to the south in winter.

A large male walrus (*overleaf*) can measure over 3.5m (12ft) and weigh 1.3 tonnes. Both sexes have tusks; they use these for digging up the seabed for shellfish, dragging themselves out of the sea on to the shore or an ice floe, keeping open breathing holes in the ice, and for fighting during the breeding season.

Penguins (*page 64*) are found south of the equator but only the Emperor and the Adélie (shown here) breed on the inhospitable shores of Antarctica, where they congregate in large colonies.

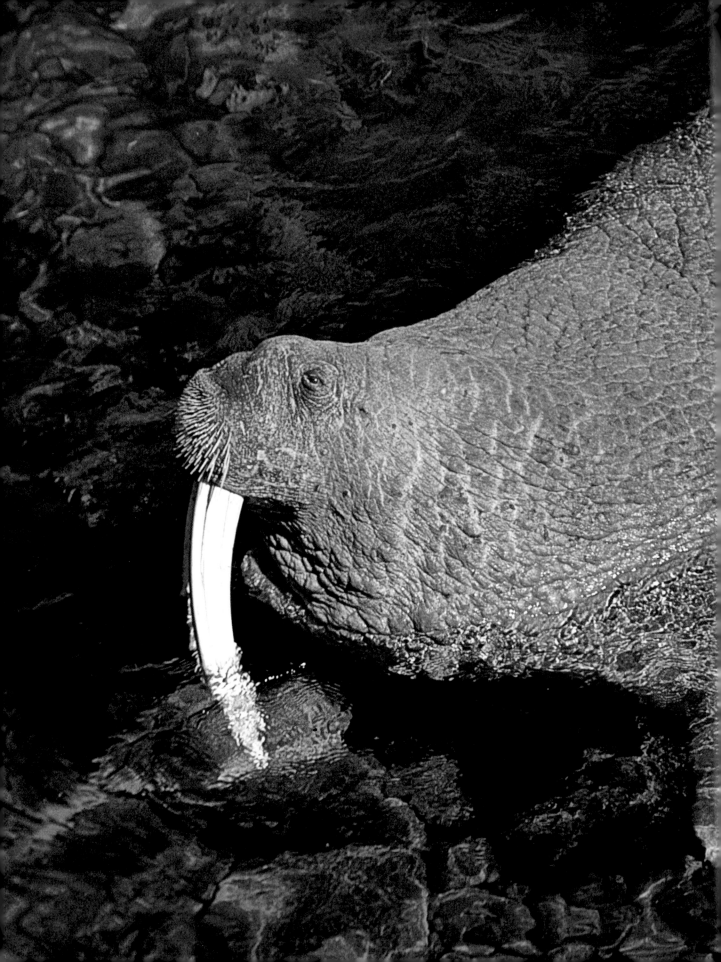

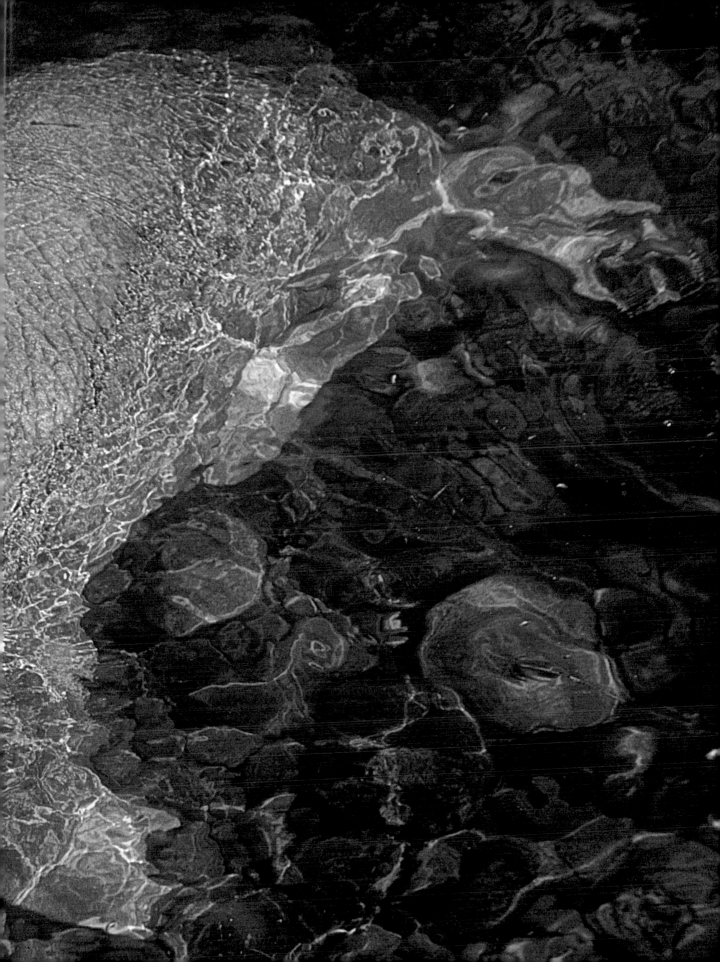

INDEX

Figures in italic refer to illustrations.

Anaconda 19, 22, 23
Anteater 19, 22, 23, 35
Antelope 42, *43*
Armadillo 4, 19, *22*

Bear, Big Brown 30, *40-1*
Bear, Grizzly 30, *31*
Bear, Polar 57, 58
Beaver 19, *28*
Birds *1*, 4, 6, *10*, 11, *18-19*, *24*, *25*, 32, 33, *36*, *37*, 41, *44*, *45*, *50*, 51, *60*, 64
Bison, American 19, *30*
Bison, European *46*
Bustard 33, 41, *45*

Caribou 58, 60, *61*
Cassowary 6, 37
Cheetah *4-5*
Cockatoo, Sulphur-crested *36*, 37
Cock-of-the-rock, Peruvian *24*
Crane, Crowned *10*, 11
Crocodile 14, *15*

Deer 4, 41, *42*

Eagle, Golden 41, *44*, 45
Elephant 4, *14*

Flamingo *1*
Fox 22, 41, *58*
Frog, Flying *52*

Giraffe 4, *16*, 17
Gorilla 7, 12, *13*, 32

Hummingbird *18-19*
Hippopotamus 4, 6, 32

Kangaroo 35, *38*
Kiwi 33, *37*
Koala 33, *34*, 35

Lion 4, *8-9*, 17

Macaw 4, *24*
Mandrill *12*
Marmoset, Golden Lion 20, *21*
Marsupials 32, 33, *34*, 35, *38*, *39*

Okapi *17*, 33
Orang-utan *2-3*, 7
Ostrich *11*, 33, 37
Otter 46, *47*
Owl, Snowy *60*

Panda, Giant 32, 33, *54-5*
Panda, Red *55*
Peacock 4, *50*, 51
Penguin 32, 33, *64*
Pheasant *51*
Platypus, Duck-billed 32, 33, 35, *38*
Polar Bear *56-7*, 58
Porcupine 28, *29*
Prairie Dog 7
Przewalski's Horse 46, *47*
Python, Reticulated 22, *52*, *53*

Raccoon 28, *29*, 54
Reptiles 14, *15*, 19, 22, 23, *52*, *53*
Rhinoceros 7, 14, *15*, 32, 33

Seal 58, 60, *61*
Secretary Bird *11*
Skunk, Striped 19, 24, *26-7*
Sloth 20

Tamarin *20*
Tapir, Malayan *54*
Tasmanian Devil 38, *39*
Tiger, Bengal *48-9*
Tiger, White 6, 7
Toucan 6, 24, *25*

Walrus 60, *62-3*
Wolf 41, 58, *59*
Wombat 35, 38, *39*

Zebra *17*
Zoo 4, 6, 7, *13*, *16*, 32-3, 54

Acknowledgements

With the exception of the following individuals and organizations the photographs for this book are provided by Bruce Coleman Ltd:
Heather Angel 38 above; Ardea, London 56-57, (Edwin Mickleburgh) 64 below; Nigel Cassidy 15 below; Spectrum Colour Library 11 below.

FRONT COVER PHOTOGRAPH: JAMES DAVIS TRAVEL PHOTOGRAPHY

This edition published in 1990 by Treasure Press, Michelin House, 81 Fulham Road, London SW3 6RB

© 1981 Octopus Books Limited

ISBN 1 85051 485 2

Produced by Mandarin Offset
Printed in Hong Kong